PRESIDENTIAL ELECTIONS IN IRAN

Changing Faces; Status Quo Policies

NATIONAL COUNCIL OF RESISTANCE OF IRAN
U.S. REPRESENTATIVE OFFICE

Presidential Elections in Iran; Changing Faces; Status Quo Policies

First published in 2017 by
National Council of Resistance of Iran - U.S. Representative Office (NCRI-US),
1747 Pennsylvania Ave., NW, Suite 1125, Washington, DC 20006

ISBN-10:   1-944942-04-1
ISBN-13:   978-1-944942-04-5

ISBN-10:   1-944942-05-X (e-book)
ISBN-13:   978-1-944942-05-2 (e-book)

Library of Congress Control Number: 2017942150
Library of Congress Cataloging-in-Publication Data

National Council of Resistance of Iran - U.S. Representative Office.
Presidential Elections in Iran; Changing Faces; Status Quo Policies

1. Iran. 2. Elections. 3. Human Rights. 4. Terrorism. 5. Revolutionary Guards

First Edition: May 2017

Printed in the United States of America

Table of Contents

Introduction

The twelfth round of presidential elections and the fifth round of city and village council elections will take place on May 19, 2017. For the presidential elections, a total of 1,636 individuals registered as candidates. The Guardian Council, made up of six clerics appointed by the supreme leader and six jurists with the power to vet candidates, approved the candidacy of only 6 people while rejecting 1,630 remaining individuals. Among the 1,630 people whose candidacies were rejected were figures like former two-term president Mahmoud Ahmadinejad, and mullah Hashem Botai, a current member of the Assembly of Experts, Mohammad Gharazi, whose candidacy was previously approved in 2013 by the Guardian Council. The list also included a number of ministers and current and former members of Parliament (Majlis). The Guardian Council provided no explanations or rationale for the rejections either to the candidates themselves or to the public at large.

Selection of Presidential Candidates in the Theocratic Regime

The Five Qualifications

Article 115 of the Constitution of the Islamic Republic of Iran states: "The President of the Republic must be elected from among the religious and political elite who meet the following qualifications: Iranian origin, Iranian nationality, administrative leadership, clear past record, honesty and piety, believing in the fundamentals of the Islamic Republic of Iran and the official religion of the country."

The determination for whether a candidate meets these five qualifications falls on the Guardian Council to select the eligible individuals to voters. Article 91 of the Constitution mandates the creation of the "Guardian Council" (*shoray-e negahban*), which is comprised of six clerics handpicked by the supreme leader (*vali-e faqih*) and six jurists appointed by the head of the judiciary, who himself is also appointed by the supreme leader.

The Guardian Council's Constitutional Violations

During the past 11 presidential elections, the Guardian Council has never vetted the candidates in accordance with Article 115. For example, in the current election cycle, there are a significant number of individuals who meet all the above qualifications. They include:

- ☑ Mahmoud Ahmadinejad, president for two terms and whose candidacy was approved previously. His candidacy was rejected in this round without any explanation.

- ☑ Mohammad Gharazi, whose presidential candidacy was approved in 2013. He campaigned alongside other candidates like Rouhani. However, his candidacy was rejected without any explanation.

- ☑ Hashem Botai, whose candidacy was approved by Guardian Council for membership in the Assembly of Experts. However, his presidential candidacy was rejected without any explanation (this is while the candidacy of another Assembly of Experts member, Ebrahim Raisi, was approved).

- ☑ During the 11th round of presidential elections, even the candidacy of Ali Akbar Hashemi Rafsanjani, who helped the regime appoint Ali Khamenei as the current supreme leader, was rejected by the Guardian Council.

Proportion of Rejected Candidacies in 12 Presidential Elections

The table below lists presidential candidates as well as the number of those approved by the Guardian Council:

	Official statistics claimed by the Iranian regime in the past presidential elections					
Round	Date of Elections	Registered Candidates	Approved Candidates	% Approved	Voter Participation	Name of President
1	January 25, 1980	124	123	99.0	67.0%	Abolhassan Banisadr
2	June 24, 1981	71	4	5.7	64.0%	Mohammad-Ali Rajai
3	October 2, 1981	46	4	8.7	64.0%	Seyyed Ali Khamenei
4	August 6, 1985	50	3	6.0	55.0%	Seyyed Ali Khamenei
5	June 28, 1989	79	2	3.3	55.0%	Ali-Akbar Hashemi Rafsanjani
6	June 11, 1993	128	4	3.1	51.0%	Ali-Akbar Hashemi Rafsanjani
7	May 23, 1997	238	4	1.6	80.0%	Mohammad Khatami
8	June 8, 2001	817	10	1.2	67.0%	Mohammad Khatami
9	June 17, 2005	1014	8	0.8	60.0%	Mahmoud Ahmadinejad
10	June 12, 2009	475	4	0.8	85.0%	Mahmoud Ahmadinejad
11	June 14, 2013	686	8	1.2	72.7%	Hassan Rouhani
12	May 19, 2017	1636	6	0.4		

The Guardian Council was not yet created during the first round of presidential elections in the clerical regime, which was established after the 1979 revolution. At the time, former supreme leader Khomeini initially announced that anyone can become a presidential candidate and the people can choose their preferred option.

However, after Mr. Massoud Rajavi, who enjoyed widespread popularity among various sectors of society, declared his candidacy, Khomeini changed his stance and declared that those who have not voted in factor of the Constitution cannot become president.

The organization led by Rajavi, the People's Mojahedin Organization of Iran (PMOI/MEK), had boycotted the vote on the Constitution due to its inclusion of the principle of *velayat-e faqih* (absolute rule of the clerics). Still, Mr. Rajavi had announced his candidacy by officially declaring compliance with the Constitution.

Supreme Leader's 4 Filters for a President

In the velayat-e faqih system, the selection of a president is controlled and vetted by the supreme leader at four stages or points. This is to ensure that the president aligns with the wishes and mandates of the supreme leader. The four filters are:

1. An unwritten rule is that all candidates who end up being approved by the Guardian Council must have received permission from the supreme leader to run for president. Without exception, any candidate who has not received Khamenei's permission has not been approved. Two specific examples are Rafsanjani's candidacy in 2013 and Ahmadinejad's in 2017:

    a. As he described in his memoirs, Rafsanjani said that he was awaiting Khamenei's response to his candidacy until the last minutes of the deadline for registration. Khamenei refused to respond to Khamenei despite repeated phone calls by Rafsanjani to Khamenei's office. When Rafsanjani finally declared his candidacy in the final stretch of registration, observers were stunned to hear that the Guardian Council, at Khamenei's direction, rejected Rafsanjani's candidacy.

    b. In September 2016, Ahmadinejad met with Khamenei to request permission to run as president. However, Khamenei suggested that he should not declare his candidacy. Khamenei later announced publicly that he had recommended to Ahmadinejad not to run in the next presidential elections. But when Ahmadinejad announced his candidacy in contradiction to Khamenei's direction, the Guardian Council rejected his candidacy without providing any explanations.

2. Vetting of candidates by Guardian Council: The Guardian Council selects a final list of presidential candidates in accordance with Article 115 of the Constitution. In ten of the last 11 presidential elections where the Guardian Council has been involved in the vetting process, the percentage of approved candidates has been in the single digits. In recent years, that number has been reduced to less than one percent. The Guardian Council completes this process not on the basis of Article 115 but based on the explicit direction of the supreme leader. In a word, in every round, candidates are approved on the basis of Khamenei's determination of his regime's interests in that particular context.

3. Engineering of elections: Among the candidates selected by Khamenei, and announced by the Guardian Council in every round, Khamenei and his faction have a stronger tendency towards some and therefore resort to organized rigging implemented by security-intelligence organizations (the Islamic Revolutionary Guard Corps, Bassij, plain clothes agents, etc.) as engineering of election results. For example, in 2005, when Rafsanjani announced his candidacy, at a time when Khamenei did not have

a tendency to agree to it, according to a self-described[1] multi-year engineering plan, enacted by the IRGC and coordinated by Brig. Gen. Baqer Zolqadr, Ahmadinejad's name appeared out of the ballot box.

4. Consenting to election: Article 110 of the Constitution of the regime proffers extensive authority to the supreme leader. For example, paragraph 9 of Article 110 of the Constitution declares that the supreme leader must approve the election of the president. Unless and until the supreme leader approves the election of the president, the president has no authority to head the executive branch. Therefore, the approval is not a symbolic function. The president's legitimacy derives from the supreme leader's final approval after the election. The approval has a supervisory mechanism until the end of the president's term. If and when the president deviates from the determined principles (opposing the *velayat-e faqih*), his legitimacy and credibility will be revoked. On

---

[1] The engineering of election results in the regime is an extremely complex and secret endeavor because it takes place against officials at the highest levels of the system. For example, in 2005, Khatami was the president and Rafsanjani was the head of the Expediency Council. Both of them had access to extensive information and intelligence. In addition, Ali Larijani was another presidential candidate who was endorsed by the Principalist council chaired by Nateq Nouri. Therefore, the engineering was a multi-layer plan, with an initial step of registration of multiple candidates to facilitate a second round of elections (since pulling Ahmadinejad, a low-tier IRGC member, out of the ballot box in competition with the likes of Rafsanjani, Larijani and Karoubi would have been too obvious and raised suspicions). As a second later, armed forces and militias, which in accordance with the law do not have the right to interfere in politics, act as a political party to organize votes. And, third, the regime employs tactics of vote rigging through the repeated participation of organized armed and security forces. They do this using fake identification cards and birth certificates of the deceased.

this basis, the final dismissal of the president occurs by the supreme leader, a logical extension of the initial approval letter, after the vote of non-confidence by the parliament or a judicial ruling by the judiciary. It was on this basis that Khomeini issued the dismissal order of the regime's first president Banisadr.

Therefore, on the basis of these four filters, the president is practically an appointee of the supreme leader and not an official elected by the populace. Even without regard to the engineered aspect of the "elections" and systematic vote rigging, the opinion and vote of the voters is essentially contained and limited to the candidates selected by the supreme leader and whose presidency is contingency on the continued approval of the supreme leader, whom has full authority to lend him legitimacy and to dismiss him.

Previous Presidents and Their Disposition

The Fate of 7 Presidents

To better understand the issue, one must look back at the previous presidents who came from various different factions.

- ☑ Banisadr: sacked and removed
- ☑ Rajai: killed
- ☑ Khamenei: transitioned to role of supreme leader
- ☑ Rafsanjani: died with a significantly diminished profile
- ☑ Khatami: dismissed as a "seditionist"
- ☑ Ahmadinejad: sidelined as a "deviant"
- ☑ Rouhani: to be determined

All Presidents Left in Conflict with the Supreme Leader

With the exception of Mohammad-Ali Rajai, who was president for a little more than a month, the other six presidents all had conflicts with the Supreme Leader. When he was president, Khamenei, who later became the supreme leader, sparred with Khomeini over the appointment of a prime minister. At the time, the president had the authority to recommend a prime minister for approval by Majlis. Khamenei was vehemently opposed to Mir Hossein Moussavi, but Khomeini imposed Moussavi on him. The conflict escalated to an extent where Khamenei only expressed agreement to run for a second term on the condition that he would have the power to select his own prime minister. Khomeini refused, which led Khamenei to avoid participating in certain meetings with Khomeini as an expression of dismay.

While Rafsanjani (1989-1997) had been instrumental in helping Khamenei climb the ladder to become the supreme leader, he clashed repeatedly with Khamenei as president in the early 1990s. The animosity between the two continued until Rafsanjani's death in early 2017. In a detailed and comprehensive analysis, the Iranian Resistance had described the pair at the time as the "contradictory but inseparable duo." The contradiction was so pronounced that in 2013 Khamenei opted to reject Rafsanjani's presidential candidacy in contradiction of the regime's own laws and customs.[2]

The next president, Mohammad Khatami (1997-2005) praised Khamenei as occupying the position usually ascribed to prophets, describing his rulings as divine orders. Currently, however, Khatami is viewed as a "seditionist" by Khamenei and his camp. The Supreme National Security Council has ordered state-run media to ban broadcasting of Khatami's images, speeches and writings.

---

[2] The conflict between Rafsanjani and Khamenei was so deep-seated that when Rafsanjani suddenly died in January 2017 that some began to view the death as suspicious and even attributed to Khamenei's faction.

Finally, Ahmadinejad (2005-2013), whom Khamenei described in a public speech on June 20, 2009 as the closest individual to him after calling him the most revolutionary figure of the regime in 2005, later in 2011 distanced himself from Khamenei after a public spat over the appointment of the intelligence minister. Ahmadinejad refused to appear in public for 11 days to show his dismay over Khamenei's decision. Now, in 2017, his presidential candidacy has been rejected and he has been threatened with house arrest and even prison.

It remains to be seen what the fate of Rouhani will be after the end of his presidential term.

The Roots of Discord and Conflict Between the President and the Supreme Leader

Despite the fact that the regime's presidents can only occupy the post after passing through the above-mentioned four filters of the supreme leader, in all of the presidential terms, there have been major clashes between the president and the supreme leader. In one instance, Khomeini faced off directly with Banisadr. In other cases, the conflicts have escalated away from the public eye. What is the root of these clashes and conflicts?

In the 1979 revolution the people of Iran were yearning freedom, liberty, independence and the republic system of governance. The population sought a democratic republic, elements of which they had experienced in various phases of their history since the

Constitutional Revolution of 1906, especially during the short-lived tenure of the nationalist Prime Minister, Dr. Mohammad Mossadeq in the early 1950s. However, Khomeini clearly hijacked the revolution and sought to implement his own theory of "Islamic Caliphate." Elaborating on his Islamic system of governance on April 28, 1984 (on the anniversary of the birth of the Prophet of Islam), Khomeini criticized himself for not announcing an Islamic Caliphate since day one of obtaining power and said: "We want caliphs to cut hands, issue sentences and stone to death."[3] In reality, Khomeini wanted an Islamic caliphate based on Islamic fundamentalism and extremism whereas the Iranian people wanted a democratic republic. In order to institute his dream, Khomeini implemented the principle of an Islamic caliphate through a velayat-e faqih in the Constitution. However, in the

---

[3] Khomeini's speech on the anniversary of the Prophet's first revelation in 1984: "The real day of God is the day when Amir al-Momenin (Ali) drew his sword and destroyed the Khavarej (deviants) from the beginning to the end and killed them all. The days of God are the days when the Lord releases an earthquake, a flood, a storm, lashes people so they can be fixed. If Ali had appeased, he would not have drawn a sword to kill 700 people at once. These are mostly the people in our prisons, who are corrupt. If we don't kill them, each one of them will kill someone when released. These people will not be fixed. ... You clerics, why do you pursue only rulings on prayer and fasting? Why do you recite the compassionate Quranic verses? Why do you avoid the verses on killings? The Quran calls on you to kill, beat and imprison. Why do you stick to the part that speaks of compassion? Compassion is against God. ... The alter is a place for war. Alters are places of war. Most of the wars in Islam arise from alters. The prophet had a sword to enable him to kill. Our imams were military personnel. They came of war. They drew their swords to kill. ... We want caliphs to cut hands, issue sentences and stone to death. Just as the prophet cut hands, issued sentences, and stoned. Just as the Jews massacred the dissident Banu Qurayza. If the prophet ordered to invade a place, to set fire on a house, to destroy a certain tribe, he has issued a just order. He issued qisas to ensure human life. The life of the masses is based on these qisas deaths. The issue will not be resolved with several years of imprisonment. Dispense with such childish sentiments." https://www.balatarin.com/permlink/2016/6/3/4201588

context of those social and historical circumstances, he could not fully dispense with the idea of a republic and elections. In 1981, he expressed regret and criticized the contradiction forming in his system of governance, saying that he made a mistake for not closing all doors after the revolution and for not eliminating all opponents.[4] (See the footnote for the audio of the speech).

The conflict between freedom and the dictatorship called the Islamic caliphate (or the absolute rule of the clergy) represents the war between the Iranian people and the ruling clerics. Since the executive branch inevitably deals with the population and while all the governments have sought to preserve the rule of the velayat-e faqih, their dealings have been murky. The Guardian Council is in fact the guardian and powerful steward of the Islamic caliphate.

---

[4]   https://www.youtube.com/watch?v=BEXdUz-CUWk

The 12th Presidential Elections

Challenges for the Supreme Leader

As the presidential elections approach on May 19, 2017, in Iran, Khamenei faces numerous challenges and crises. Most important among them are three main crises, which will force Khamenei to acquiesce to one of the candidates:

1. Fear of another popular uprising: Despite years of brutal suppression, deliberations within the regime still consider a popular uprising as an existential threat. Leaders of the Khamenei faction explicitly refer to this threat in their speeches. For example, Heydar Moslehi, a former intelligence minister (Moslehi was the subject of Khamenei's clash with Ahmadinejad in 2011). On April 16, 2017, Moslehi told a gathering of Bassij militias at Tehran's Aminollah base with respect to the current circumstances: "The enemy is still plotting to create a sedition and sedition is certain."[5] He added that the elections must take place in a way that prevents the threat of uprisings.

   On May 10, 2017, Supreme Leader Ali Khamenei, addressing a graduating cadets of the Islamic Revolutionary Guards Corps, emphasized that security was the most important issue

---

[5] Regime officials describe the uprisings as "sedition" (e.g. the "sedition of 2009").

in the May 19 election. "National security and the country's tranquility is important, and the honorable candidates must be careful not to instigate geographical, lingual and ethnic divisions and not play in the hands of the enemy. If anyone seeks to take measures against the country's security, they will most definitely receive a slap in the face," he said. "If people break the law and gain hope through the enemy's words, the elections will be against our interests... The country's security must remain untouched," the Supreme Leader emphasized.[6]

---

[6] "Iran Leader Vows 'Slap in the Face' for Election Disruptions," The New York Times, May 10, 2017, https://www.nytimes.com/2017/05/10/world/middleeast/khamenei-iran-election-warning.html
Also see: http://ncr-iran.org/en/news/election/22767-khamenei-anyone-acting-against-national-security-will-receive-slap-in-the-face

2. The crisis of succession: Many speculate that Khamenei will die in the next four years in view of his health and his age. Therefore, the various factions within the regime seek a president who will ensure Khamenei's legacy in the share of power.

3. Changes in the international political climate following the U.S. elections have meant that one-way concessions to Khamenei, who continues to pursue the nuclear program, exporting terrorism and suppression at home, have not ceased.

In addition to these crises, Khamenei faces a significant fissure within his own camp after the 2009 uprisings and his diminishing role. Fissures and defections within Khamenei's camp, which represents the political cover for the suppressive and security forces operating under the political umbrella of "principlists," have significantly accelerated and deepened. Following the weakening of the supreme leader after the 2009 uprisings, and after the regime's retreat during the 2015 nuclear deal, Khamenei is in a vulnerable position. He has lost his position within the regime as the determining force. His agents and followers are being pulled in every direction (the most significant of which was Ahmadinejad, who refused to acquiesce to Khamenei's explicit orders and still registered as a presidential candidate).

Latest Situation and Prospects

☑ Among the six candidates, the highest probability of victory belongs to Rouhani, Raisi or Qalibaf. Jahangiri will in all probability drop out in favor of Rouhani. The two remaining candidates, Mirsalim and Hashemitaba do not have a chance at winning. Mirsalim's presence created a fissure in the coalition of popular forces of the Islamic Revolution (JAMNA).[7] The Motalefeh, which was a main force in the JAMNA coalition, and one of the 10 founders of which was the deputy of the Motalefeh, Asadollah Badamchian, decided to support Mirsalim (and not JAMNA candidates Raisi or Qalibaf) despite the fact that the coalition did not choose Mirsalim as its preferred candidate.

☑ The Khamenei faction has been split into the following four camps:

1) Avoid participation: Ahmadinejad supporters

2) Raisi-Qalibaf supporters: JAMNA (suppressive forces)

3) Mirsalim supporters (Motalefeh)

4) Rouhani supporters (fundamentalists supporting Rouhani)[8]

☑ Hassan Rouhani and Jahangiri asked for Khamenei's permission in February 2017. Rouhani stated that if Khamenei has someone else in mind, he would drop out as

---

[7] JAMNA was formed several months ago with the aim of creating unity among various Khamenei factions to support a single presidential candidate.

[8] The leaders of this faction are Nateq Nouri, Ali Larijani, Ali Motahari, and a number of the Society of Struggling Clerics and clergy in Qom.

an "insignificant soldier." In the end, Khamenei accepted both of their candidacies.

☑ The Islamic Revolutionary Guard Corps (IRGC) and JAMNA coalition want Raisi to become president. Raisi made his candidacy contingent on Khamenei's approval. Khamenei approved his candidacy in March 2017.

☑ Qalibaf had initiated his campaign a year before the elections. After the IRGC and Khamenei supported Raisi, Qalibaf refused to register as a candidate. However, Khamenei's office asked him on the fourth day of registrations to sign up. The plan was for him to appear in presidential debates and to make revelations against Rouhani. At the same time, Raisi was to be portrayed as a non-partisan actor. Qalibaf would opt out in favor of Raisi. He registered as a candidate on the fifth day of registrations.

☑ The topic of a shadow candidate for Rouhani became apparent a long time ago. Rouhani had disapproved of the idea. However, when Qalibaf announced his candidacy as an opponent of Rouhani in the final hours of the registration, Jahangiri also announced his candidacy (as a Rouhani supporter).

☑ As such, the Rouhani-Jahangiri camp stands against Raisi-Qalibaf duo in the elections. Mirsalim and Hashemitaba are not considered serious candidates. Khamenei has stage managed this rivalry in order to portray that there is real competition in the elections. He wants a large voter turnout in order to convince the international community that the clerical regime enjoys popular legitimacy. Meanwhile, all the candidates are approved and cleared by Khamenei himself.

- ☑ With respect to the stage-managed show of displaying a high voter turnout, the regime has extensive schemes, which includes bringing foreign reporters to specific polling stations on Election Day. The regime's supporters and agents would form long lines at those polling stations, and would prevent these foreign reporters to browse in Tehran and other large cities. Domestic reporters would face threats and intimidation while covering other stations. At the same time, the regime will add mobile polling station ballots in order to increase the number of the ballots.

- ☑ The IRGC has created a significant number of fake identification cards. It has also worked with the intelligence organization of the IRGC to identify deceased people in order to use their IDs to vote.

- ☑ As for the final vote tally, consistent with past practice, the votes for each candidate will be proportionally increased four or five-fold to show a high voter turnout.

History of Eleven Elections and Seven Presidents

First Presidential Election – January 1980

Iran's first presidential election was held on January 25, 1980, a year after the revolution. At the time, the Council of the Revolution was running the country following the resignation of the provisional government of Mehdi Bazargan.

Candidates

There were 124 candidates in the first round of the presidential election, but after the withdrawal or resignation of some candidates, eventually the field was reduced to 96. The Guardian Council had not yet been formed, and Khomeini had declared that in this election, anyone could run, i.e. no one would be disqualified. The most well-known candidates were Abolhassan Banisadr, Ahmad Madani, Dariush Forouhar, Sadegh Ghotbzadeh, Massoud Rajavi, Hassan Habibi, Kazem Sami, Hassan Ayat, Sadeq Tabatabai, Sadeq Khalkhali, Mohammad Mokri, Safar Ali Khalili.

The leader of the People's Mojahedin Organization of Iran (PMOI/MEK), Massoud Rajavi, arguably the most recognizable

Abolhassan Banisadr

Massoud Rajavi

Dariush Forouhar

Hassan Habibi

Kazem Sami

Ahmad Madani

Sadegh Ghotbzadeh

Sadeq Tabatabai

face among the candidates, had announced a 12- point platform, which attracted the support of a wide range of people of diverse social and ethnic backgrounds.

The MEK had opposed the insertion of "the principle of *velayat-e faqih*" (absolute rule of a jurisprudent deemed Supreme Leader) into the Constitution, regarding it as the most important barrier to freedom. Its removal became one of the movement's conditions for participation in the constitutional referendum, and when that did not happen, the MEK advocated a boycott of the referendum on the Constitution.

Faced with the widespread support for Rajavi's candidacy, Khomeini and his supporters took the threat of his election seriously. Although Rajavi had run with a commitment to the Constitution as adopted, Khomeini violated his own declaration and in a statement on January 19, 1980, declared that "those who did not vote for the Constitution of the Islamic Republic are not eligible to become Iran's president." After his disqualification, the first to occur in a presidential election, Mr. Rajavi wrote in a message to the Iranian people: "Now more than anything else I think about the fate of the Revolution that has put one of history's greatest responsibilities on my shoulders and that of my sisters and brothers."

Ultimately, the presidential election was held on January 25, and Abolhassan Banisadr was elected as the first president of the clerical regime. Banisadr's term in office lasted less than 17 months. Khomeini could not tolerate him, and he was deposed on June 20, 1981.

Second Presidential Election – August 1981

Since Banisadr's term remained unfinished, and the country was being run by the presidential council, a second presidential election was held in August 1981.

Candidates

This time around, 71 candidates registered, 67 of whom were disqualified by the newly formed Guardian Council. The four who did qualify were Mohammad Ali Rajai, Abbas Sheibani, Habibollah Asgaroladi and Ali Akbar Parvaresh.

Muhammad Ali Rajai was elected as President, but his term in office lasted less than a month because on August 30, 1981, Rajai

| Mohammad Ali Rajai | Abbas Sheibani | Habibollah Asgaroladi | Ali Akbar Parvaresh |

and his Prime Minister, Mohammad Javad Bahonar, were killed in a bomb explosion during a meeting of the Security Council of the Islamic Republic in the Prime Minister's boardroom.

Third Presidential Election – October 1981

The third presidential election saw 46 candidates register, 42 of whom were disqualified by the Guardian Council. The finalists were: Seyyed Ali Khamenei, Seyyed Ali Akbar Parvaresh, Hassan Ghafourifard and Seyyed Reza Zavarei.

Prior to this election, Khomeini had opposed the participation of the clergy in executive positions, especially the presidency. This time around, he reversed this opposition, allowing Khamenei to run and ultimately win the election.

Seyyed Ali Khamenei

Hassan Ghafourifard

Seyyed Ali Akbar Parvaresh

Seyyed Reza Zavarei

Fourth Presidential Election – August 1985

Seyyed Ali Khamenei

Habibollah Asgaroladi

Seyyed Mahmoud Kashani

The fourth presidential election in Iran was held on August 16, 1985. Fifty candidates had registered, but the Guardian Council approved only three and disqualified the rest. The trio consisted of Khamenei, Habibollah Asgaroladi and Seyyed Mahmoud Kashani. The most famous among the disqualified was Mehdi Bazargan, the first Prime Minister of the Provisional Government, who had been appointed by Khomeini and his government called the "Government of Imam Mahdi" (12th Shiite Imam). The disqualification of Bazargan sparked protests.

Some of the religious authorities in Qom, among them Mohammad Kazem Shariatmadari, Seyyed Shahabeddin Marashi Najafi and Mohammad Sadegh Rouhani also boycotted the elections.

Khamenei became President for a second term.

Fifth Presidential Election – August 1989

Iran's fifth presidential election and the first election after Khomeini's death was held on July 28, 1989. 790 people had registered to run, but 11 withdrew and the Guardian Council approved only two candidates of the remaining 779. 777 were disqualified.

Ali Akbar Hashemi Rafsanjani

The two candidates deemed eligible by the Guardian Council were Ali Akbar Hashemi Rafsanjani and Abbas Sheibani. Rafsanjani was elected as President.

Abbas Sheibani

Sixth Presidential Election – June 1993

Ali Akbar Hashemi Rafsanjani

Doctor Abdullah Jafarali Jassbi

Ahmad Tavakoli

In the sixth presidential election, 128 people registered to run and the Guardian Council, in what had by now become its custom, disqualified 124 of them. Ali Akbar Hashemi Rafsanjani, Doctor Abdullah Jafarali Jassbi (President of Azad University), Rajab Ali Taheri (Representative of Kazeroun in the first parliament) and Ahmad Tavakoli were allowed to run. Jassbi and Taheri were supporters of Rafsanjani; only Ahmad Tavakoli was considered as Rafsanjani's rival.

Rafsanjani was again elected as President.

Seventh Presidential Election – May 1997

Iran's seventh presidential election was held on May 23, 1997. Of the 238 who registered, 234 were disqualified, leaving only four eligible to run. They were: Seyyed Mohammad Khatami (former minister of Culture and Islamic Guidance), Ali Akbar Nateq Nouri (Speaker of Parliament), Reza Zavarei (head of Organization for Registration of Deeds and Properties), and Mohammad Mohammadi Reyshahri (former Minister of Intelligence).

About 8 months before the election, Mohammad Khatami had gone to see Khamenei, who had taken over as Supreme Leader after Khomeini's death in 1989, and asked his permission to run for the presidency. Khamenei had agreed, since he had no doubt about Khatami's loyalty to the regime of *velayat-e faqih*.

Seyyed Mohammad Khatami

Ali Akbar Nateq Nouri

Mohammad Mohammadi Reyshahri

Seyyed Reza Zavarei

In this election, the Islamic Revolutionary Guards and Ministry of Intelligence (then run by Minister Ali Fallahian and his Deputy for Internal Security Saeed Imami) as well as Supreme Leader Khamenei favored Nateq Nouri. Brigadier General Baqer Zolghadr the IRGC's acting commander, even campaigned for Nateq Nouri, but contrary to expectations, Mohammad Khatami was elected. Hours before the results were announced, Nateq Nouri had already congratulated him.

Incumbent President Hashemi Rafsanjani, who favored Khatami, had become aware of behind-the-scene plans by the IRGC to rig the results. One week before the election, Rafsanjani announced in the Friday Prayers in Tehran that he would prevent any fraud. This was a blow to the IRGC's planned election engineering, and despite the fact that in some provinces (including the Central Province) the number of votes cast for Nateq Nouri was higher than for other candidates, Khatami was elected. Those voting for Khatami generally wanted to cast a negative vote against Nateq Nouri, who they saw as Supreme Leader Khamenei's candidate, rather than a positive vote for Khatami.

Eighth Presidential Election – May 2001

In the eighth presidential election in Iran, 817 candidates registered, 807 of them were disqualified by the Guardian Council, and 10 were declared eligible. This marked the first time that ten people were declared eligible candidates. The inclusion of nine people running against Mohammad Khatami was part of a scheme by the IRGC and Khamenei faction to prevent Khatami from winning.

The slate included Mohammad Khatami, Ahmad Tavakoli, Ali Shamkhani, Abdullah Jassbi, Hassan Ghafourifard, Mansour Razavi,

Seyyed Mohammad Khatami

Ali Fallahian

Mahmoud Kashani

Ahmad Tavakoli

Ali Shamkhani

Abdullah Jassbi

Shahabeddin Sadr, Ali Fallahian, Mostafa Hashemitaba and Mahmoud Kashani.

The IRGC and security forces of Khamenei's faction had faced a major dilemma with the election of Khatami, especially because of the high turnout due to revelations of serial killings inside Iran associated with the Guards and security forces. Therefore, in their overall scheme for this election, the nine other candidates, some of whom (including HashemiTaba and Shamkhani) were in Khatami's cabinet, were brought in to break up the vote for Khatami. Despite widespread election engineering and fraud, the hatred of the Khamenei faction was such that Khatami again won the vote.

Ninth Presidential Election – June 2005

The ninth presidential election in the Islamic Republic was held on June 17, 2005. It was the first to lead to a second ballot. In the runoff held on June 24, Mahmoud Ahmadinejad was elected.

In this election, 1014 people registered to run, and the Guardian Council approved six and disqualified 1008. Two of the disqualified candidates, Mostafa Moein (Khatami's Science Minister) and Mohsen Mehr-Alizadeh (Khatami's deputy) sought and received a special dispensation from Khamenei allowing them to run, bringing the number to eight candidates for the election: Mahmoud Ahmadinejad, Ali Akbar Hashemi Rafsanjani, Mehdi Karroubi, Mohammad Bagher Qalibaf, Mostafa Moein, Ali Larijani and Mohsen Mehr Alizadeh.

Mahmoud Ahmadinejad

Ali Akbar Hashemi Rafsanjani

Mehdi Karroubi

Mostafa Moein

Ali Larijani   Mohsen Mehr Alizadeh   Mohammad Bagher Qalibaf

The election marked the most complex presidential election-engineering by the ruling regime in the past 11 rounds. Khamenei had decided to purge Rafsanjani, always his rival and the regime's number-two. He also decided to get rid of Karroubi, the Speaker of the Parliament beloved by Khomeini; Ali Larijani, the candidate of the traditional right (later called the Pricipalists), and Qalibaf, another conservative candidate, in favor of a low-ranking Revolutionary Guard named Ahmadinejad.

Brigadier General Mohammad Baqer Zolghadr was one of the key designers of this rigging scheme, later referred to it as multi-layer election engineering. One layer was to encourage some of the so-called reformists to run alongside Rafsanjani. Another layer was to misdirect the public, in such a way that it was made to look as if the favored candidates of the Principlists were Ali Larijani and Qalibaf. Meanwhile, the *Bassij* storm troopers and security forces were organized to vote for Mahmoud Ahmadinejad.

Accordingly, none of the candidates received the necessary 50 percent of the total in the first round. At this stage, the following voter tallies were declared:

Rafsanjani	Ahmadinejad	Karroubi
6,211,937	5,711,696	5,070,114

Gradually, as the votes were counted, Karroubi's tally exceeded Ahmadinejad's, contrary to the expectations of the conspirators. They were forced to change the numbers, making Ahmadinejad's tally higher and Karroubi's lower.

Karroubi issued an open letter, accusing Mojtaba Khamenei (the Supreme Leader's son), the IRGC, *Bassij* and the Guardian Council of election fraud: "Around 3:00 AM on Saturday, June 18, when the official recording of the votes at the election site began, all official statistics were showing my votes much higher than other respected candidates. At 5:00 AM, when I went for a rest, I had about 25 percent of the votes and other candidates had less than twenty percent ... but after about two hours of sleep, when I woke up, I realized that everything had changed ... About half past eight in the morning, I contacted the Interior Ministry officials and they too expressed surprise at the action of the Guardian Council and radio and television."

In other words, even after all the engineering, if it were not for this last act of fraud, Karroubi and Rafsanjani would have gone to the second round. Instead, Rafsanjani and Ahmadinejad went to the second round.

After more fraud in the second round, Ahmadinejad was declared President. Rafsanjani issued a statement about "election fraud" and said because of the "incompetence of observers (appointed by the Guardian Council) in handling complaints... I am complaining to God."

He added: "I believe non-electoral tools were used. Whatever one wants to call it. I consider it vote manipulation, vote replacement and use of governmental facilities as non-electoral tools. If you can show me a country where in two elections, seven million votes become seventeen million, and twenty million become ten million, I will take you at your word."

Elaheh Koulaee, spokesperson of Mostafa Moein, read a statement from this candidate in the Participation Front headquarters, saying, "a military and paramilitary process" had influenced the result. The Special Inspector of the Interior Ministry was detained for several hours for protesting the actions of the Guardian Council observers and the situation at polling stations.

The Interior Ministry, as election administrator, stopped the voting process because of fraud in some electoral districts, but the Guardian Council intervened to prevent the vote from being halted.

Keyhan newspaper acknowledged the rigging in an article about meetings of political directors of the IRGC, writing: "Besides the spectrum of voters, there is a set of decision-makers and political activists who have played a major role in bringing about the auspicious phenomenon of June 24. This set is still as powerful as in the past, but livelier than before on the scene, and in any challenge in the future will have an important role. Without any intention of restricting this set to a particular group, only as an indicator, we can assume that organizations such as the Student *Bassij*, mobilization of students, mobilization of teachers and urban and rural areas of Bassij were one of the main pillars of how the votes came out on June 24."

Tenth Presidential Election – June 2009

Iran's tenth presidential election was held on Friday, June 12, 2009. In this election, 475 people registered, the Guardian Council disqualified 471 people and qualified 4 candidates: Mahmoud Ahmadinejad, Mir Hossein Moussavi, Mehdi Karroubi and Mohsen Rezai.

All four candidates had received Khamenei's blessing before the election. Following the ninth election and the disclosures made by Rafsanjani, Karroubi, the reformists and even people from the Khamenei faction such as Nateq Nouri, Khamenei decided to completely remove all of them—Rafsanjani, Moussavi, Karroubi, and the reformist faction.

A social climate of revulsion was created in reaction to the Ahmadinejad/Khamenei gang, with the controversial disclosures that Khamenei had launched through Ahmadinejad to hammer Rafsanjani, Karroubi, Nateq Nouri and Mir Hossein Moussavi. That atmosphere became more active, tilting the vote in favor of Moussavi, to the extent that Ali Larijani, Speaker of the Parliament, congratulated Mir Hossein Moussavi on his victory before the official announcement of the results.

Mahmoud Ah-
madinejad

Mir Hossein
Moussavi

Mehdi Karroubi

Mohsen Rezai

But Ahmadinejad's Interior Ministry announced election results of about 24 million votes for Ahmadinejad, 13 million for Mir Hossein Moussavi and even less for Mehdi Karroubi, declaring Ahmadinejad as President in the first round! When the candidates complained about the fraud, the Iranian people poured into the streets to voice their demands, shouting: "The election is an excuse, the whole system is the target," and called for its overthrow.

Eleventh Presidential Election – June 2013

The eleventh Iranian presidential election was held on June 14, 2013. Some 686 people registered, of whom 678 were disqualified and 8 were allowed to run: Hassan Rouhani, Mohammad Reza Aref, Mohammad Bagher Qalibaf, Saeed Jalili, Ali Akbar Velayati, Haddad Adel, Mohsen Rezai and Mohammad Gharazi. Later Aref resigned in favor of Rouhani, and Haddad Adel resigned in favor of the Principlists' candidate.

The most important disqualified candidate was Ali Akbar Hashemi Rafsanjani, the second in command of the regime during the Khomeini era and the man responsible for the choice of Khamenei as Supreme Leader. Khamenei had decided to prevent the emergence of Rafsanjani and his faction at any cost, to the extent of disqualifying Rafsanjani!

The Khamenei faction calculated that after Rafsanjani was disqualified, he would not support Rouhani and Rouhani would not get the vote. Therefore, to maintain outward appearances, the Guardian Council approved Rouhani along with Mohammad Reza Aref, never predicting that after Rafsanjani, Aref would withdraw in favor of Rouhani. But Rafsanjani entered into the

Hassan Rouhani

Mohammad Bagher Qalibaf

Saeed Jalili

Ali Akbar Velayati

Mohammad Gharazi

Mohsen Rezai

fray, with a specific plan against Khamenei, and engineered Aref's withdrawal in time.

Khamenei's faction tried hard to get the four Principlist candidates, Qalibaf, Saeed Jalili, Haddad Adel and Ali Akbar Velayati, as well as Mohsen Rezai to withdraw in favor of the candidate leading in the polls. But except for Haddad Adel, the others failed to do so.

On the other hand, Khamenei had seen to it that the Guardian Council rejected Rafsanjani. He did not want to overplay his hand, creating an excuse for another uprising.

This set of circumstances resulted in Rouhani's election as the regime's eleventh President.

Biographies of 2017 Presidential Candidates

Biography of Hassan Rouhani,

Current Iranian President and Presidential Candidate for the 2017 Election

Name: Hassan

Last name: Rouhani

Former name: Hassan Fereidoon (Changed name to Rouhani, which means "spiritual" or "cleric")

Birth: 12 November 1948 in the City of Sarkheh (Semnan Province)

Education: BA in Judicial Law, Tehran University (1972) M.Phil. Degree in Law, Glasgow Caledonian University (1995) Ph.D. in Constitutional Law, Glasgow Caledonian University (1999) Married: Married his cousin Sahebeh Arabi (Rouhani), who is six years younger Children: 4 children. His eldest son committed suicide in 1992.

- ☑ 1986: Member of the High Council for War Support (1986-1988) Head of the Executive Committee (1986-1988) 1989Appointed member of the Supreme National Security Council (SNSC) by Supreme Leader Khamenei

- National Security Adviser to the President Hashemi Rafsanjani (1989-1997) 1998: Elected member of the Council of Experts (selects Supreme Leader and oversees actions)
- Member of the Presiding Board and Head of the Office of the Council of Expert's Secretariat (2006-2008) 2000: Re-elected to the Council of Experts, Head of the Political and Social Committee
- National Security Adviser to the President (Mohammad Khatami)
- 2003: Appointed top nuclear negotiator October 2003
- 2013: Elected president (Combatant Clergy Association political party)

From the very beginning of the rule of the mullahs on Iran, Hassan Rouhani became close to Rafsanjani and has always been amongst the regime's officials, being alongside Rafsanjani during the 8-year war with Iraq and in the regime's Majlis (parliament). He also has had a first-degree role in all of the regime's crimes.

Khomeini

Rouhani first met Ayatollah Khomeini in 1963, likely after his arrest by the Shah. In early spring, the Shah had attacked Iran's mullahs, calling them "black reactionaries." In response, Khomeini delivered a scathing speech, describing the Shah as a "poor miserable creature." He raised the possibility that the Shah might actually be an Israeli and a Jew.

Khomeini's attack on the Shah led to his house arrest for eight months in a suburb of Tehran. Here, he met a "stream of militants," likely including Rouhani, who had been first arrested in 1962 and was making speeches against the government.

Rouhani was monitored by SAVAK. Ayatollahs Mohammad Beheshti and Morteza Motahhari urged Rouhani to leave Iran to avoid being jailed. For 18 months, Rouhani went abroad, giving speeches to Iranian students at universities.

Rouhani formed a close bond with Khomeini and was asked to deliver the sermon at Khomeini's son's memorial service in November 1977.

Rouhani was reportedly influential in publicizing the title of "imam" for Khomeini. The title historically had been used only with Ali, the fourth Caliph, and his 11 male descendants. Khomeini was the first to also claim the title in 12 centuries.

When Khomeini was exiled to Paris, Rouhani travelled to France to be with him.

Roles and Government

Among his other responsibilities in the clerical regime, Rouhani has been Khamenei's representative at the Supreme National Security Council, member of the Expediency Council, Tehran's representative in the Council of Experts and the head of Strategic Research Center of the Expediency Council. According to his own confessions, Rouhani is one of regime's highest security officials. He was the head of the Supreme National Security Council from 1989 to 2005, which lead dozens of political assassinations outside Iran. The number of executions in Rouhani's term exceeded 3000 people, which has been even higher than Ahmadinejad's presidential term. During his term in office, many security officials and torturers participated in the decision making bodies, including Mostafa Pour Mohammadi, who is the current Minister of Justice and one of the main members of the death committee in the 1988 massacre of 30,000 political prisoners. Some other torturers and security leaders in his government, who are also engaged in his election campaign for 2017, are as follows:

Name	Position in government	Security background
Hassan Rouhani	President	The head of the Supreme National Security Council/commander of the air defense during the 8 year war
Hossein Fereidoon	Brother of the president and special assistant	Intelligence Ministry
Ali Rabi'i	Minister of Labor, Cooperation and Social Welfare	Member of the prime minister's intelligence/ deputy of the Intelligence Ministry/ Supreme National Security Council

Name	Position in government	Security background
Hamid Chitchiyan	Minister of Power and Electricity	Deputy of the Intelligence Ministry
Ali Younessi	President's special assistant in family relations	Intelligence Minister during Khatami's presidency
Hessamoddin Ashna	President's cultural consultant	Intelligence Ministry
Mostafa Pour Mohammadi	Minister of Justice	Deputy of Intelligence Ministry
Abbas Ahmad Akhoundi	Minister of Roads	Security deputy of the Interior Ministry
Rahmani Fazli	Minister of Interior	Member of the Supreme National Security Council
Reza Salehi Amiri	Minister of Islamic Culture and Guidance	Deputy of the Intelligence Ministry
Mohammad Bagher Nobakht	Spokesman of Rouhani's government	Torturer and murderer in the City of Rasht

Name	Position in government	Security background
Mohammad Shariat-madari	The executive assistant to the current government and the election campaign leader of Hassan Rouhani	Leaders of the Islamic revolutionary committees in 1979 and head of the intelligence and security. Morteza Haji, who is the leader of the reformist election campaign, was among the notorious torturers in Mazandaran Province.

Supreme National Security Council

The Supreme National Security Council (SNSC) (aka Supreme Security Council) was established in a referendum that approved amendments to Iran's Constitution in July 1989. The SNSC is Iran's top decision-making body, charged with 'overseeing defense and state security policy as well as coordinating the activities of various defense and intelligence bodies.

Supreme Leader Khamenei appointed Rouhani a member of the Council in September 1989 and tasked him with helping set up the organization. Rouhani served on the Council until August 2005, following the election of Mahmoud Ahmadinejad.

Hashemi Rafsanjani, elected president in July 1989, also was a founding member of the SNSC.

The SNSC's membership includes:

- ☑ Heads of Executive, Legislative, and Judiciary branches of government
- ☑ Chief of the Supreme Command Council of the Armed Forces
- ☑ Head in charge of the Plan and Budget Organization
- ☑ Two representatives nominated by the Supreme Leader
- ☑ Minister of Foreign Affairs
- ☑ Minister of Intelligence and Security
- ☑ Chief of the Supreme Command Council of the Armed Forces
- ☑ Chief of the Army
- ☑ Chief of the Islamic Revolution's Guards Corps

Top Nuclear Negotiator

Rouhani was appointed the head of Iran's nuclear negotiating team on October 6, 2003, several weeks after the International Atomic Energy Agency (IAEA) issued a report, stating Iran was concealing nuclear enrichment and reprocessing activities.

Under IAEA rules, the findings of the report should have been referred to the UN Security Council for consideration of sanctions. Instead, the IAEA issued a series of demands to rectify Iran's breaches.

Rouhani, then Secretary of Iran's Supreme National Security Council (SNSC), the top decision-making body on security issues, stepped into the breach and took over negotiations with the IAEA. He remained at this post until August 15, 2005, when he resigned, following the election of Mahmoud Ahmadinejad as President of Iran. Below is an overview of Iran's nuclear events during Rouhani's tenure as head nuclear negotiator.

Several months after stepping down as Iran's nuclear negotiator, Rouhani disclosed in a speech how he had duped the west during nuclear negotiations, keeping Iran's nuclear program on track while avoiding referral to the UN Security Council for possible sanctions.

Rouhani's speech was published in the fall of 2005 by Rahbord. At the time, Rouhani was managing editor of Rahbord, published by the Center for Strategic Research.

In those remarks, Rouhani boasted that "while talks were taking place in Tehran, Iran was able to complete the installation of equipment for conversion of yellowcake – a key stage in the nuclear fuel process – at its Isfahan plant but at the same time convince European diplomats that nothing was afoot."

Below are excerpts from Rouhani's speech.

The Dilemma

"In a meeting of the state's leaders at 2003, it was discussed that according to the IAEA resolution of September 2003, we had to provide a complete picture of our nuclear activities of previous years to the IAEA.... The dilemma was if we offered a complete picture, the picture itself could lead us to the UN Security Council. And not providing a complete picture would also be a violation of the resolution and we could have been referred to the Security Council for not implementing the resolution."

Partners Informed IAEA

"Most of the activities that we had carried out and had not informed the IAEA about them were reported to the IAEA by countries that were our partners in those activities. For instance, we had implemented some plans with the Chinese and according to the safeguard regulations we had to report them to the IAEA and we had not done so. These were reported to the IAEA by the Chinese and they told us that they had informed the IAEA. In addition, the Russians had also already informed the IAEA of some of the equipment that we had purchased from them."

Suspensions and Technical Difficulties

"Another issue that was raised was the fact that the Europeans gradually realized that we did not accept suspension in the areas that we had technical difficulties and only agreed to suspension in the areas that we faced no technical problems. This is a point that they point out to in the talks recently. For instance, we completed

Isfahan that is the section for U.C.F. and the factory that converts yellow cake to UF4 and UF6 was completed during the suspension period. When we were negotiating with Europeans in Tehran, we were still installing some of the equipment in Isfahan site and there was plenty of work to be done to complete this site and finish the work there. In reality, by creating a tame situation, we could finish Isfahan."

Fait Accompli

"I should tell you that we need some time to implement our capabilities. I mean if we could complete the fuel cycle and make it fait- accompli for the world, then the whole situation would be different."

After Rouhani's speech was published, Ali Akbari, a regime strategist close to Supreme Leader Ali Khamenei, accused Rouhani of divulging state secrets that would lead to its referral to the UN Security Council.

Biography of Ebrahim Raisi

Name: Ebrahim

Last name: Rais os-Sadati

Also known as: Ebrahim Raisi

Birth: 1960 in the city of Mashhad

Education: 6th grade, religious and clerical studies

Raisi is the son-in-law of the Ayatollah Ahmad Alam-Alhoda, the Friday Prayer of Mashhad, northeast Iran.

Raisi is one of Supreme Leader Ali Khamenei's disciples and was under his tutelage from 1991 to 2001. It is believed he is being groomed to be a leading candidate to succeed Ali Khamenei.

A Look Into Raisi's Background

After completing grade 6 at the age of 15, Mullah Raisi continued his education on clerical studies first in Mashhad and then in Haghani School in the City of Qom. He had only completed 3 years of clerical studies when the 1979 revolution took place in

Iran. Despite his lack of knowledge of the regime's own sharia, Mullah Beheshti selected him as a member of the suppressive judicial system right in the beginning of the revolution, along with other brutal clerics, Ali Fallahian, Ruhollah Hosseinian, and Mostafa Pourmohammadi.

As Khomeini's reign began, Raisi was invited and went to the City of Masjid Soleiman, by Mullah Hadi Marvi, Khomeini's representative in that city, and with his minimum knowledge of the judicial matters, he started suppressing dissidents and leftist groups.

A year after his involvement in the suppression of the people of Masjid Soleiman, while he was only 19 years old, he was sent to Karaj as a prosecutor, where he started the interrogation and torture of young dissidents. A year later, Ali Qoddusi, the Revolutionary Prosecutor at the time, appointed Raisi at the age of 20 as the prosecutor general in the city of Karaj (west of Tehran). Several months later, Raisi was promoted and became the prosecutor general for the city of Hamadan, western Iran, where he remained as the city's prosecutor until the 1984. In that position, he was directly responsible for the execution of hundreds of political activists in the city.

In 1984, Ali Razini replaced Assadollah Lajevardi as the country's Revolutionary Prosecutor. He brought Raisi from Hamadan to Tehran and appointed him as the Revolutionary Prosecutor's deputy.

Raisi became the country's assistant prosecutor at the age of 24. In that position, he was directly responsible for the death of thousands of dissidents, especially the activists of the

Mujahedin-e Khalq (PMOI/MEK). In 1988, he was one of the three members of the "Death Committee," which ordered the execution of 30,000 political prisoners, already serving time, in a matter of a few months.

At the time, Ayatollah Hossein-Ali Montazeri described that massacre as the "greatest crime" committed by the Islamic republic.

Raisi was appointed as Tehran's Revolutionary Prosecutor in 1989. He was the Head of the Office of the Inspector General for a decade from 1994 to 2004. Since 2012, while he held the position of Deputy Head of Judiciary, upon Khamenei's order, he became the Prosecutor General of the Special Court for the Clergy, charged with disciplining dissident clerics.

In 2006, he was elected to the Assembly of Experts that has powers to choose the next supreme leader, and now sits on its board of directors.

He was appointed by Khamenei as the custodian of Astan-e Qods Razavi, the largest religious endowment in Iran, in 2016. The custodian of the shrine is one of the most powerful people in Iran, as he oversees the holiest site in Iran — which also engages in major economic activities.[9]

Raisi has been among the top brass of the regime Judiciary, where he played a direct role in the suppression of the 2009 uprising. He was Iran's prosecutor general until 2016.

With the approval of Khamenei, Raisi allocated a significant portion of Qods Razavi's revenues to the terrorist Qods Force

---

[9] See The Rise of the Revolutionary Guards' Financial Empire, published by the National Council of Resistance of Iran-U.S. Representative Office, March 2016, page 84. https://www.amazon.com/Irans-Revolutionary-Guards-Financial-Empire/dp/1944942025/

of the Islamic Revolutionary Guard Corps (IRGC), including its extensive meddling in Syria, Yemen and Iraq. For this reason, he has the full backing of Majors General Qassem Soleimani, the Qods Force Commander, and Mohammad Ali Jafari, the IRGC Commander-in-Chief.

On 6 April 2017, Raisi announced his official nomination for the upcoming presidential election. He registered on April 14.

Biography and Background of Mohammad Baqir Qalibaf

First name: Mohammad Baqir

Last Name: Qalibaf

Birth: August 23, 1961 in the town of Torqabeh, near the provincial capital of Mashhad

Education: PhD in political geography at Tarbiat Modarres University (received his degree from the Revolutionary Guards (IRGC)). He is also known to have undergone Airbus pilot training in France. And member of the scientific delegation and assistant professor of the human geography group in the Geography College of Tehran University.

Mohammad Baqir Qalibaf, the current mayor of Tehran, registered as a candidate from Supreme Leader Ali Khamenei's faction, the Principlists, on April 15, 2017. He was among the 6 candidates approved by the Guardian Council on April 20, 2017.

A Summary of Qalibaf's Role in Suppression

Simultaneous with the revolution in 1979, Qalibaf began his activities in the Bassij paramilitary. he was involved in the suppression of uprisings in Kurdistan Province. He became a member of the Islamic Revolutionary Guard Corps (IRGC) since its formation in Khorassan Province in the 1980s. He went to the frontlines as the Iran-Iraq War broke out in 1980. He e was the Brigade commander of Imam Reza Unit in 1982 and the fifth Division commander of Khorassan Nasr in 1983.

Qalibaf participated in many of the regime's attacks during the war and personally sent many youth and children to the minefields. In 1987, he was first appointed as the deputy commander of the IRGC Moqaddam Compound in the West of the country and then as the commander of Najaf Compound in Kermanshah, where he remained until the end of the war in 1988. As the war subsided, he became the commander of section 3 of the country and played a leading role in the crackdown of Iran's northern provinces of Gilan and Mazandaran. He was then appointed as the commander of Karbala 25 brigade in Mazandaran Province and finally became the head of the IRGC ground forces in 1990.

In 1991, he moved on to the IRGC Joint Headquarters Coordination Office until being promoted in 1994 to deputy commander on the Khatam Al-Anbia Construction Company, a large construction firm affiliated with the IRGC. That same year, Qalibaf was transferred and appointed as the Bassij deputy commander where he played an active role in crackdowns and established bases associated to the "Headquarters of Promoting Virtue and Prohibiting Vice," an entity known for its gross human rights violations.

Qalibaf is also known as one of the main elements behind establishing Bassij intelligence teams aimed at identifying resistance activists, arresting dissidents and imposing harsh punishments and restrictions on personal freedoms.

In 1997, he moved on to become the IRGC Air Force commander, replacing Brigadier General Jalali. He served in this post until the year 2000 and was active in the IRGC missile units. He was involved in expanding the teams from three surface-to-surface missile units to five brigades, and mainly focusing on further developing the Shahab ballistic missile. On June 27, 2000, Khamenei appointed Ghalibaf as commander of Iran's State Security Forces (SSF) to replace Brigadier General Lotfiyan. Over the next three years, he commanded the SSF to suppress popular dissent and opposition movements. Ghalibaf expanded the police anti-riot units, established state police border posts and launched the repressive "110 Police" units. He also imposed several fundamental changes in the SSF organizational structure and allocated huge budgets to provide these organs with more equipment used in popular suppression.

In a widely-distributed recording in early 2013, Qalibaf is heard boasting to the Bassij militia about ordering police to open fire on student demonstrators in 2003 and of personally attacking students with a wooden baton in an earlier demonstration in 1999.He also took credit for helping to suppress the 2009 post-election demonstrations in his role as Tehran mayor.

As the commander of SSF in 2003, he claimed that by making harsh statements and intimidating members of Iran's Supreme National Security Council, he managed to obtain permission to shoot at student protesters. "In that meeting, through my behavior, I was able to get permission from the country's security council for the police forces to have a military presence at the university dorm and shoot [at protesters]," he said.

Qalibaf appointed Azizollah Rajabzadeh, the commander of the Ministry of Intelligence in Tehran, one of the participants of the Kahrizak detention center and attacks on Tehran University Dormitory on June 15, 2009, as the head of the prevention and management of crisis organization in Tehran.

He is now serving his second term as Tehran's mayor since his first election in 2005.

A very close friend of Qalibaf is cleric Hassan Kurdmihan. He is one of the main people responsible for attacking the Saudi Arabian embassy in Tehran in January 2016. Kurdmihan is a well-known figure in Qalibaf's election campaign. He also led his election campaign in Karaj in 2013.

Under his supervision, there are 4 large bases for the Bassij Forces called "Nour Maarefat Religious and Cultural Institution" in Karaj, "Behesht Religious – Cultural Institution" in Tehran, "Imam Mohammad Baqir Religious Center" in Tehran and "Heyat ol Reza" in Karaj. These bases have access to large funding sources to spread pro-state propaganda.

Biography and Background of Eshaq Jahangiri

First Deputy of Rouhani and Candidate for the Presidential Elections

First name: Eshaq

Last name: Jahangiri

Birth: January 21, 1958 in Sirjan County, Kerman Province

Education: Graduated from University of Kerman with a degree in physics; he later received a PhD from Islamic Azad University, Science and Research Branch in industrial management

On April 15, 2017, Eshaq Jahangiri, Rouhani's first vice president, appeared at the Interior Ministry and registered as a candidate for the 2017 presidential election. The Guardian Council later vetted and approved Jahangiri's candidacy.

Background

☑ Appointed deputy head of the agriculture department in Kerman in July 1980

- ☑ Head of the agriculture department in Kerman in 1982
- ☑ Member of Parliament in 1984
- ☑ Appointed governor of Isfahan in 1992 by then-president Ali Akbar Hashemi Rafsanjani
- ☑ Nominated by Mohammad Khatami as the minister of mines and metals in 1997. His portfolio was later changed to the minister of industries and mines
- ☑ Co-founded Executives of Construction Party and served as its secretary general from 2006 to 2010
- ☑ He was also a member of Mir-Hossein Moussavi's presidential campaign in 2009 presidential election
- ☑ Appointed as the First Vice President to Rouhani in 2013

Jahangiri is affiliated with factions close to former president Ali Akbar Hashemi Rafsanjani. He is among the founding members of the Executives of Construction party. Jahangiri was the representative of Jiroft in the second and third terms of the parliament and the mayor of Isfahan for a while. He was also a member of the science delegation from the "Rain" foundation (affiliated with Mohammad Khatami). Rouhani appointed Eshaq Jahangiri as his first deputy on August 5, 2013.

Jahangiri had two brothers who were members of the Islamic Revolutionary Guard Corps (IRGC) and were killed during the 8-year war with Iraq. During the conflict, Jahangiri was in charge of the war effort in Kerman and actively sent forces into the battle fields. He is very close to Qassem Soleimani, the commander of the IRGC extraterritorial Qods Force.

According to the state-affiliated Fars news agency in October 2015, Jahangiri was introduced as the representative of the investment company of Iran's Meli Bank for the management delegation of Sadra Company affiliated with the IRGC. Sadra Company is considered to be one of the largest financial cartels of the IRGC and is active in implementing large investment plans, especially in water works projects, bridges, harbors and the oil Industry.

He was a member of the science delegation of the Industrial management organization during Mahmoud Ahmadinejad's first term in office.

Jahangiri met with Khamenei in March 2013. He then appeared at a TV program called "identification," which aired on channel 3 of Iran's state-run TV on March 15, 2013 and said: "We are getting close to the 2013 presidential elections and everything we have is the leader who can talk about our problems. We requested to see him and he humbly accepted our visit and we spoke." He added: "He (Khamenei) particularly emphasized on distancing ourselves with those who do not accept the Islamic Republic."

Biography of Seyyed Mostafa Mirsalim

First name: Seyyed Mostafa

Last name: Mirsalim

Birth: June 9, 1947, Tehran

Education: B.Sc. in Mechanics from Universite de Poitiers in 1969; M.Sc. in Mechanics from École nationale supérieure de mécanique et d'aérotechnique, 1971.

Mirsalim registered as a candidate for the 2017 presidential elections on April 11 as a representative of the traditionalist and reactionary faction of Motalefeh. His candidacy was later approved by the Guardian Council.

Following the 1979 revolution, Mirsalim headed the propaganda section of the newly established Iranian regime's "Islamic Republic" party (from 1979 to 1981). Since 1993, he became a member of the central council of the Islamic Motalefeh party. He is currently a well-known representative figure of this faction. In October 2015, the eleventh assembly of the Motalefeh elected him as part of its 30-member central council. He is currently the head of the central council of Motalefeh.

Previous Responsibilities

Mirsalim is one of the very few post-revolution figures who occupied a government-affiliated post during the Shah's era. In 1975, after he returned to Iran from France, he began to teach at the Tehran Polytechnic University. Following the 1979 uprisings against the monarchy, he was active in forming and training the first armed groups of the Islamic Revolutionary Guard Corps (IRGC). In early 1980, then-Interior Minister Mahdavi Kani appointed him as the chief of police in addition to retaining his responsibilities as the head of the political and social office of the interior ministry.

Mirsalim was appointed Minister of Culture and Islamic Guidance in 1994. The Ministry under his direction was particularly known for closing down a number of newspapers.

Over the past 20 years, Mirsalim has been somewhat out of the political limelight. He is a member of the Expediency Council, but he is more known for his non-political activities than his political status. For example, he has grabbed headlines for seeking to produce a national car engine at a large car manufacturer. Still, he has retained a prominent advisory role to the regime's highest officials throughout the years.

Biography of
Mostafa Hashemitaba

First name: Mostafa

Last name: Hashemitaba

Birth: May 22, 1946 in Isfahan

Mostafa Hashemitaba was the minister of industries in the early years of the 1979 revolution (in the government of Mohammad Javad Bahonar). He was the chair of the Physical Education Organization during the second term of the presidency of Ali Akbar Hashemi Rafsanjani (1993 to 1997) as well as in the first term of Mohammad Khatami's presidency (1997 to 2001). He was also the head of the National Olympic Committee of Iran.

In March 2015, he was appointed by Mohammad Goudarzi, the Minister of Youth Affairs and Sports, as an advisor for infrastructure, investments and expansion of athletic opportunities.

He also ran in the eighth round of presidential elections in 2001 against Mohammad Khatami. He placed last among approved candidates, earning just a little over 28,000 votes.

About NCRI-US

National Council of Resistance of Iran-US Representative Office acts as the Washington office for Iran's Parliament-in-exile, which is dedicated to the establishment of a democratic, secular, non-nuclear republic in Iran.

NCRI-US, registered as a non-profit tax-exempt organization, has been instrumental in exposing many nuclear sites of Iran, including the sites in Natanz, and Arak, the biological and chemical weapons program of Iran, as well as its ambitious ballistic missile program.

NCRI-US has also exposed the terrorist network of the Iranian regime, including its involvement in the bombing of Khobar Towers in Saudi Arabia, the Jewish Community Center in Argentina, its fueling of sectarian violence in Iraq and Syria, and its malign activities in other parts of the Middle East.

Visit our website at **www.ncrius.org**

You may follow us on   **twitter** 🐦   @ncrius

Follow us on      NCRIUS

You can also find us on      NCRIUS

www.ingramcontent.com/pod-product-compliance
Lightning Source LLC
Chambersburg PA
CBHW051248020426
42333CB00025B/3117